First World War
and Army of Occupation
War Diary
France, Belgium and Germany

58 DIVISION
174 Infantry Brigade
London Regiment
2/5 Battalion
1 September 1915 - 22 February 1916

WO95/3005/1

The Naval & Military Press Ltd
www.nmarchive.com
Published in association with The National Archives

Published by

The Naval & Military Press Ltd

Unit 10 Ridgewood Industrial Park,

Uckfield, East Sussex,

TN22 5QE England

Tel: +44 (0) 1825 749494

www.naval-military-press.com

www.nmarchive.com

This diary has been reprinted in facsimile from the original. Any imperfections are inevitably reproduced and the quality may fall short of modern type and cartographic standards.

© Crown Copyright
Images reproduced by permission of The National Archives, London, England, 2015.

Contents

Document type	Place/Title	Date From	Date To
Heading	WO95/3005/1		
Heading	58th Division 174th Infy Bde 2-5th Bn London Regt 1915 Sep-1916 Feb And 1917 Jan-1918 Jan		
War Diary	Ipswich	01/09/1915	30/09/1915
Miscellaneous	War Diary Statement 2/5th City Of London Battn	01/09/1915	01/09/1915
War Diary	Ipswich	13/10/1915	22/02/1916

WO 95/30051

58TH DIVISION
174RD INFY BDE

2-5TH. BN LONDON REGT
~~JAN 1917 - JAN 1918~~

1915 SEP — 1916 FEB   (D K)
AND
1917 JAN — 1918 JAN

DISBANDED

WAR DIARY 17/8 1/5 City of London
or
INTELLIGENCE SUMMARY London Rifle Brigade

Army Form C. 2118

Page 1

(Erase heading not required.)

Place	Date 1915	Hour	Summary of Events and Information	Remarks and references to Appendices
Ipswich	Sept 1		Company & Platoon Training. 7.7.	
"	2		Battalion Emergency Training Practice (Entraining) - Company & Platoon Training 7.7.	
"	3		Company & Platoon Training. 7.7.	
"	4		Company & Platoon Training. 7.7.	
"	5		Church Parade. 7.7.	
"	6		Company & Platoon Training. 7.7.	
"	7		Company & Platoon Training - 190 officers & men (120 to shoot, remainder for supervision & butts) proceeded to Bawdsey range, Felixstowe, for musketry, returning same evening. 7.7.	
"	8		Battalion inspected at work by Genl Broadwood. 190 officers & men (120 to shoot, remainder for supervision & butts) proceeded to Bawdsey range for musketry, returning same evening. Warning of Zeppelin raid received 7.25 pm, whereon troops took up appointed stations, returning to billets about 2 am 9/9/15. 7.7.	
"	9		Company & Platoon Training. Warning of Zeppelin raid received 8.45 pm whereupon troops took up appointed stations, returning to billets about 2 am 10/9/15. 7.7.	
"	10		Company & Platoon Training. 7.7.	
"	11		Company & Platoon Training. Warning of Zeppelin raid received 10 pm whereupon troops took up appointed stations, returning to billets about 3 am 12/9/15. 7.7.	
"	12		Church Parade. 7.7.	
"	13		Company & Platoon Training. 7.7.	
"	14		Brigade operations. 7.7.	
"	15		Company & Platoon Training - Warning of Air Raid received 8.30 pm - Road Picquets took post till midnight. 7.7.	
"	16		Battalion Training	

Army Form C. 2118.

1/2/5 City of London
London Rifle Brigade
Page 2

WAR DIARY
INTELLIGENCE SUMMARY
(Erase heading not required.)

Instructions regarding War Diaries and Intelligence Summaries are contained in F. S. Regs, Part II. and the Staff Manual respectively. Title pages will be prepared in manuscript.

Hour, Date, Place		Summary of Events and Information	Remarks and references to Appendices
Ipswich	Sept 17 1915	Company & Platoon Training 7.7.	
"	18	Company & Platoon Training - Modified Period of Vigilance began 6.15 pm 7.7.	
"	19	Orders to move received 4.24 am — whole battalion was entrained at 6 am (the required time), having had breakfast. Battalion moved to Halesworth, taking up position there, returning to Ipswich in afternoon. Period of Vigilance ended 3.15 pm. Draft of 80 men proceeded by the 9.32 am train to Southampton to join the 1st Battalion overseas - 7.7.	
"	20	Company & Platoon Training 7.7.	
"	21	Company & Platoon Training -	
"	22	Company & Platoon Training 7.7. One Company marched to Bawdsey 21/9/15 (Bivouacing there) for training purposes, returning 23/9/15 7.7.	
"	23	Battalion Training 7.7	
"	24	Company & Platoon Training 7.7.	
"	25	Company & Platoon Training 7.7.	
"	26	Church Parade 7.7.	
"	27	Company & Platoon Training 7.7.	
"	28	Company & Platoon Training 7.7.	
"	29	Company & Platoon Training 7.7.	
"	30	Company & Platoon Training 7.7.	

Confidential

58th (LONDON) DIVISION — 3 SEP 1915 — GENERAL STAFF

War Diary Statement

2/5th City of London Batt.

1. Training has progressed satisfactorily.

2. Special attention has been paid to –
   a. Bayonet fighting with service bayonet.
   b. Trench digging.
   c. Night work.
   d. Miniature Rifle Range practice.
   e. Physical drill.
   f. Care of feet.

3. The officer instructional staff is good and still improving.

4. Companies were turned out several times during the month by night to take up anti Zeppelin posts, the work was well and quietly carried out.

5. One draft of 17 N.C.O.s & men went to join the 1st Batt. overseas.

G. R. Fox

Ipswich
1/9/15

Army Form C. 2118

WAR DIARY of 2/5 City of London London Rifle Brigade
INTELLIGENCE SUMMARY

(Erase heading not required.)

Instructions regarding War Diaries and Intelligence Summaries are contained in F.S. Regs., Part II. and the Staff Manual respectively. Title Pages will be prepared in manuscript.

Place	Date	Hour	Summary of Events and Information	Remarks and references to Appendices
IPSWICH	1915 Oct 13		Warning of Air Raid received at 7.25 P.m. Pickets took post remaining out till dawn	7.7.
	" 14		Battalion Training (Concentration Route March, "Digging in") Informal inspection by G.O.C. 1st Army during Training	7.7.
	" 18 19 20		75 Officers & other ranks (42 to shoot, remainder for supervision (butts) proceeded to Melton for musketry, returning each evening	7.7.
	" 22		Divisional Training	7.7.
	" 29		Divisional Training	7.7.

3 - NOV 1915

Army Form C. 2118

WAR DIARY of 2/5 City of London (London Rifle Brigade)

INTELLIGENCE SUMMARY

(Erase heading not required.)

Place	Date	Hour	Summary of Events and Information	Remarks and references to Appendices
Ipswich	1915 Nov 2/6 inclusive		Brigade march through SUFFOLK, with operations en route. This Battalion was billeted in EARL SOHAM on the night of the 2nd, in LAXFIELD on the 3rd, in HALESWORTH on the 4th, and in UFFORD on the 5th, returning to IPSWICH on the 6th inst.	7.7.
"	11		Divisional Tactical Exercise from 3 pm to 8 pm	7.7.
"	15/17 inclusive		Musketry party to Felixstowe, returning daily. (60 to fire).	7.7.
"	16		Brigade Exercise from 9 am to 5 pm.	7.7.
"	26		Divisional Exercise 9 am to 3 pm	7.7.
"	30		Brigade Operations from 9 am to 4.30 pm	7.7.

Lieut. Colonel
Commanding 2/5th City of London Batt.
(London Rifle Brigade)

Army Form C. 2118

WAR DIARY of 2/5 City of London (London Rifle Brigade)

INTELLIGENCE SUMMARY

(Erase heading not required.)

Place	Date	Hour	Summary of Events and Information	Remarks and references to Appendices
Ipswich	1915 Dec 9th		Divisional Operations 9 am to 3.30 pm FF.	[stamp: 58th (LONDON) DIVISION 2-JAN.1916 GENERAL STAFF]
"	14th		Brigade Operation 9 am to 3 pm FF.	
"	19/23		2 officers & 64 NCOs men to BUTLEY on detachment duty in connection with defence works - returned 23/12/15 FF.	
"	28		Divisional Inspection FF.	
"	22/31		1 officer & 6 men to observation post WARREN HEATH FF.	
"	28		Lt Col G.R. Tod proceeded to FRANCE, returning early January FF.	

[signature] Lieut Col Commanding

Army Form C. 2118

WAR DIARY
INTELLIGENCE SUMMARY of 2/5 City of London London Rifle Brigade
(Erase heading not required.)

Place	Date	Hour	Summary of Events and Information	Remarks and references to Appendices
IPSWICH	1916 Jan 17		6 officers transferred from 3/5 City of London to complete establishment	Nil
"	28		2 Companies took up anti-aircraft positions including road-picqueting from 9.30 pm to 12 midnight	Nil

Stamp: 58th (LONDON) DIVISION GENERAL 3 FEB 1916

WAR DIARY of 2/5 City of London Army Form C. 2118
London Rifle Brigade

INTELLIGENCE SUMMARY

(Erase heading not required.)

Place	Date	Hour	Summary of Events and Information	Remarks and references to Appendices
			for February 1916	
IPSWICH	1916 Feby 4th		244 Recruits transferred to this battalion from 3/5 City of London at Fovant, Salisbury.	
"	22nd		23 Men (formerly Home Service) rejoined from 101st Provisional Battalion, having signed A.F. E.624